Exploring Earth's Resources

Learning from Fossils

Sharon Katz Cooper

www.raintreepublishers.co.uk
Visit our website to find out more information about **Raintree** books.

To order:
☎ Phone 44 (0) 1865 888112
▤ Send a fax to 44 (0) 1865 314091
▣ Visit the Raintree Bookshop at **www.raintreepublishers.co.uk** to browse our catalogue and order online.

First published in Great Britain by Raintree, Halley Court, Jordan Hill, Oxford OX2 8EJ, part of Harcourt Education.
Raintree is a registered trademark of Harcourt Education Ltd.

Editorial: Isabel Thomas, Sarah Chappelow and Vicki Yates
Design: Michelle Lisseter
Illustrations: Q2A Solutions
Picture Research: Erica Newbery
Production: Duncan Gilbert
Originated by Modern Age
Printed and bound in China by South China Printing Company

10 digit ISBN 1 406 20623 7
13 digit ISBN 978-1-4062-0623-4
11 10 09 08 07
10 9 8 7 6 5 4 3 2 1

British Library Cataloguing in Publication Data
Cooper, Sharon Katz
    Fossils. – (Exploring Earth's resources)
    1. Fossils – Juvenile literature
    I. Title
    560

    ISBN – 13: 9781406206234
    ISBN – 10: 1406206237

A full catalogue record for this book is available from the British Library.

Acknowledgements
The publishers would like to thank the following for permission to reproduce photographs: Alamy pp. 4 (Gary Crabbe), 5 (Jill Stephenson), 21 (Heather Angel); Corbis pp. 6 (Jonathan Blair), 8 (Louie Psihoyos), 14 (Richard T. Nowitz), 17 (Layne Kennedy), 22 (Louie Psihoyos); GeoScience Features Picture Library pp. 13 (Wade Hughes), 15 (David Bayliss); Getty Images pp. 22 (altrendo nature); Science Photo Library pp. 9 (Manfred Kage), 10 (Vaughan Fleming), 11 (Michael Marten), 18 (Sinclair Stammers), 19 (Jim Amos), 20 (D. Van Ravenswaay), 16 (Ted Kinsman), 22 (British Antarctic Survey), 22 (Sinclair Stammers)

Cover photograph reproduced with permission of Corbis (James L.Amos).

Contents

Some words are shown in bold, **like this**.
You can find them in the glossary on page 23.

What are fossils?

Fossils are all that is left of plants and animals that lived a long time ago.

Dinosaur bones are fossils.

These footprints are also fossils.

Dinosaurs left them behind.

How are fossils formed?

Fossils are formed when animals die and are buried in mud.

Some fossils are formed when an animal leaves a footprint in mud.

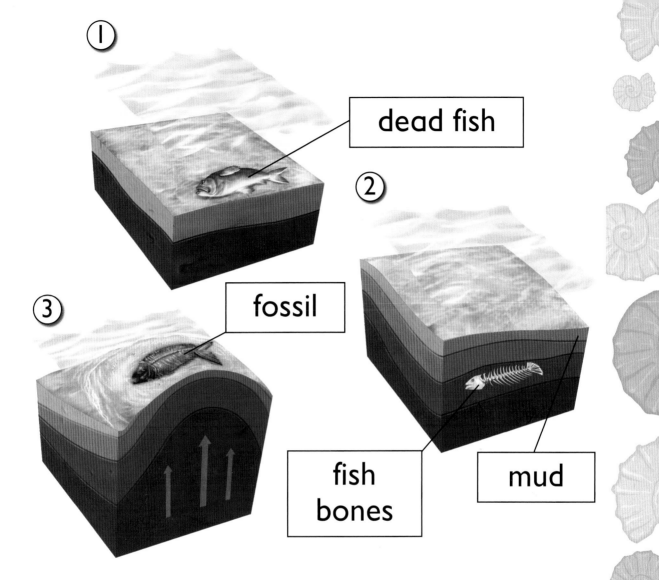

① dead fish

② fossil

③ fish bones

mud

Over a very long time, the mud becomes rock.

The animal's bones, or footprints, turn into rocks. These rocks are fossils.

Are there different types of fossils?

There are fossils of many different plants and animals.

Some are huge, like this leg bone of a dinosaur.

Actual size ↓

Other fossils are tiny. We need a **microscope** to see them.

This animal was about the size of the full stop at the end of this sentence.

Where do we find fossils?

We often find fossils inside layers of rocks.

We find them all around the world.

cliff

There are many fossils in cliffs.

These cliffs were underwater a long time ago.

We also find fossils at the bottom of the ocean.

This ship drills down into the mud and rock at the bottom of the ocean.

It brings up pieces of very old mud.

This mud holds many tiny fossils.
The fossils are the remains of
sea creatures.

Who studies fossils?

These scientists find and study fossils.

They are called **geologists** and **palaeontologists**.

These scientists study rocks and look for good places to find fossils.

How do scientists collect fossils?

Palaeontologists use large tools to remove heavy rocks.

They use small tools to dig around a fossil.

They are careful not to break the fossil.

The fossil is wrapped up. It is taken to a **laboratory** to be studied.

What can we learn from fossils?

Fossils can tell us about animals that no longer live on Earth.

These dinosaur egg fossils can tell us how dinosaurs had babies.

Fossils can tell us what **extinct** plants and animals looked like.

Look at the patterns in the rock. This dinosaur must have had feathers.

Fossils help us find out what happened in the past.

Scientists think a large **asteroid** hit Earth 65 million years ago.

The asteroid caused dinosaurs and other animals to become **extinct**.

Scientists learned this from studying tiny fossils.

Fossil quiz

There are many different kinds of fossils. Which of these photos show a fossil? (Answer on page 24.)

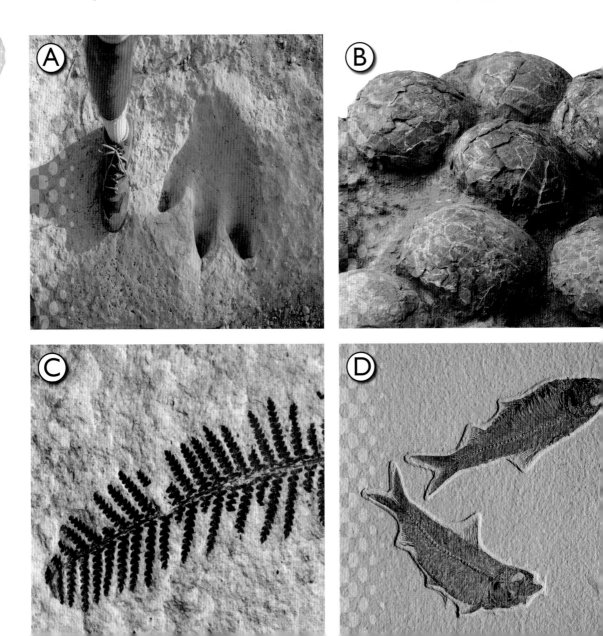

A

B

C

D

Glossary

 **asteroid** a rock from space

 **extinct** not living on Earth anymore

 **geologist** a scientist who studies rock

 **laboratory** a room where a scientist works

 **microscope** an object you use to make tiny objects look much bigger

 **palaeontologist** a scientist who finds and studies fossils

Index

Answers to quiz on page 22
All four pictures show fossils.
Photo A shows a fossil of a footprint.
Photo B shows a fossil of dinosaur eggs.
Photo C shows a fossil of a plant.
Photo D shows a fossil of fish.

Titles in the *Exploring Earth's Resources* series include:

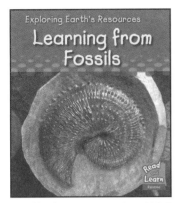

Hardback   1-406-20623-7

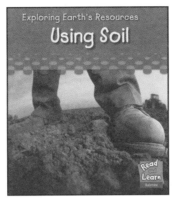

Hardback   1-406-20618-0

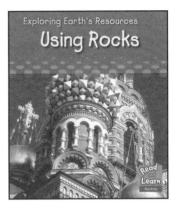

Hardback   1-406-20617-2

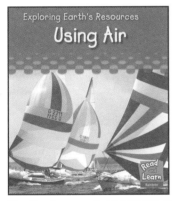

Hardback   1-406-20621-0

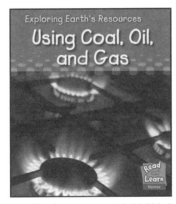

Hardback   1-406-20622-9

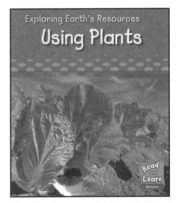

Hardback   1-406-20619-9

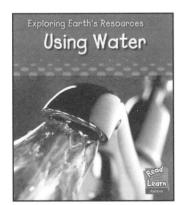

Hardback   1-406-20620-2

Find out about the other titles in this series on our website www.raintreepublishers.co.uk